SCIENCEWORKS!

Be a Demolition Engineer

By David Dreier

Demolition Consultant: Thomas J. Doud

Series Consultant: Kirk A. Janowiak

Gareth Stevens
Publishing

Please visit our web site at www.garethstevens.com. For a free catalog describing our list of high-quality books, call 1-800-542-2595 (USA) or 1-800-387-3178 (Canada). Our fax: 1-877-542-2596

Library of Congress Cataloging-in-Publication Data
Dreier, David.
    Be a demolition engineer / David Dreier.
       p. cm. —(Scienceworks!)
    Includes index.
    ISBN-13: 978-0-8368-8934-5 (lib. bdg.)
    ISBN-10: 0-8368-8934-7 (lib. bdg.)
    ISBN-13: 978-0-8368-8941-3 (softcover)
    ISBN-10: 0-8368-8941-X (softcover)
    1. Wrecking—Juvenile literature. 2. Structural engineering—Vocational guidance—Juvenile literature. I. Title.
    TH447.D75   2008
    690'.26—dc22   2007043117

This North American edition first published in 2008 by
Gareth Stevens Publishing
A Weekly Reader® Company
1 Reader's Digest Road
Pleasantville, NY 10570-7000 USA

This U.S. edition copyright © 2008 by Gareth Stevens, Inc. Original edition copyright © 2007 by ticktock Media Ltd.
First published in Great Britain in 2007 by ticktock Media Ltd., Unit 2, Orchard Business Centre, North Farm Road,
Tunbridge Wells, Kent, TN2 3XF United Kingdom

ticktock Project Editor: Joe Harris
ticktock Designer: James Powell
With thanks to: Sara Greasley and Hayley Terry

Gareth Stevens Editor: Jayne Keedle
Gareth Stevens Creative Director: Lisa Donovan
Gareth Stevens Senior Designer: Keith Plechaty

DAVID DREIER

David L. Dreier (B.S., journalism) is a freelance science writer. He spent much of his career at World Book Publishing in Chicago, Illinois, including six years as managing editor of *Science Year*, World Book's science and technology annual. He has also worked as a science reporter for a metropolitan daily newspaper, the San Antonio *Express-News*. In addition to writing about science, David has a great interest in history and has written a number of historical articles.

KIRK A. JANOWIAK

Kirk A. Janowiak (B.S. Biology & Natural Resources, M.S. Ecology & Animal Behavior, M.S. Science Education) has enjoyed teaching students from pre-school through college. He has been awarded the National Association of Biology Teachers' Outstanding Biology Teacher Award and was honored to be a finalist for the Presidential Award for Excellence in Math & Science Teaching. Kirk currently teaches Biology and Environmental Science and enjoys a wide range of interests from music to the art of roasting coffee.

THOMAS J. DOUD

Thomas J. Doud III is Project Manager of Explosives Operations at Controlled Demolition Incorporated (CDI). He has worked on a multitude of high-rise office buildings, bridges, chimneys, and industrial maintenance blasting projects undertaken by CDI both in the United States and internationally. He began work with CDI as a laborer in 1989, and has since been blaster-in-charge of numerous projects. Thom is a member of the Institute of Explosive Engineers.

CONTENTS

HOW TO USE THIS BOOK   4–5

WHAT GOES UP...   6–7

THE CHALLENGE   8–9

TOXIC MATERIALS   10–11

WRECKING BALL   12–13

HYDRAULIC EXCAVATORS   14–15

OPERATING AN EXCAVATOR   16–17

DEBRIS AND RECYCLING   18–19

PLANNING AN EXPLOSION   20–21

PLACING EXPLOSIVES   22–23

PROTECTING THE PUBLIC   24–25

A REAL BLAST!   26–27

WRAPPING IT UP   28–29

TIPS AND ANSWERS   30–31

GLOSSARY   32

This book will help students develop these vital science skills:

- Asking questions about objects, organisms, and events in the environment
- Employing simple equipment and tools to gather data and extend the senses
- Using data to construct a reasonable explanation
- Communicating investigations and explanations
- Identifying properties of objects and materials
- Identifying position and motion of objects
- Identifying a simple problem
- Proposing a solution
- Implementing proposed solutions
- Evaluating a product or design
- Communicating a problem, design, and solution
- Understanding about science and technology
- Distinguishing between natural objects and objects made by humans
- Understanding personal health
- Using science and technology in local challenges
- Understanding science as a human endeavor

Supports the National Science Education Standards (NSES) for Grades K-4

HOW TO USE THIS BOOK

Science is important in the lives of people everywhere. We use science at home and at school. In fact, we use science all the time. You need to know science to understand how the world works. A demolition expert needs to understand science to bring down buildings safely and quickly. With this book, you'll use science to plan and complete the demolition of two buildings.

This exciting science book is very easy to use. Check out what's inside!

INTRODUCTION

Do you have what it takes to be a demolition expert? Find out as you learn how to take down buildings!

FACTFILE

Read easy-to-understand information about how demolition works.

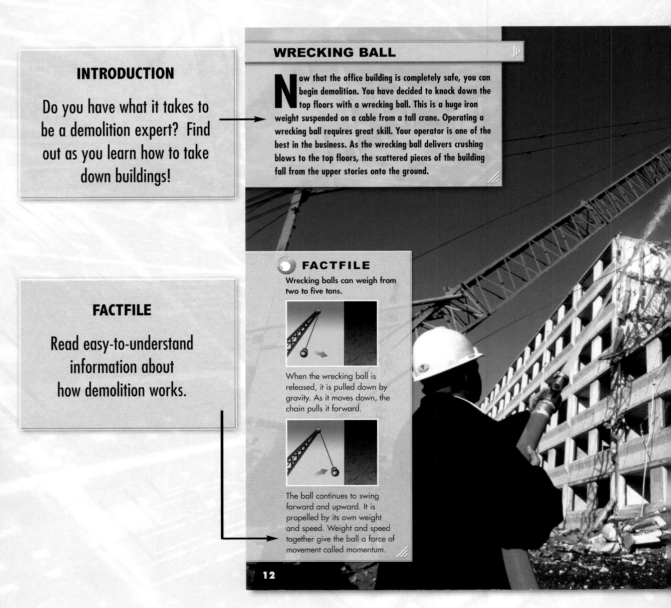

WRECKING BALL

Now that the office building is completely safe, you can begin demolition. You have decided to knock down the top floors with a wrecking ball. This is a huge iron weight suspended on a cable from a tall crane. Operating a wrecking ball requires great skill. Your operator is one of the best in the business. As the wrecking ball delivers crushing blows to the top floors, the scattered pieces of the building fall from the upper stories onto the ground.

FACTFILE

Wrecking balls can weigh from two to five tons.

When the wrecking ball is released, it is pulled down by gravity. As it moves down, the chain pulls it forward.

The ball continues to swing forward and upward. It is propelled by its own weight and speed. Weight and speed together give the ball a force of movement called momentum.

12

WORKSTATION

Learn how to interpret demolition-related data using diagrams, charts, graphs, and maps.

CHALLENGE QUESTIONS

Now that you understand the science, put it into practice.

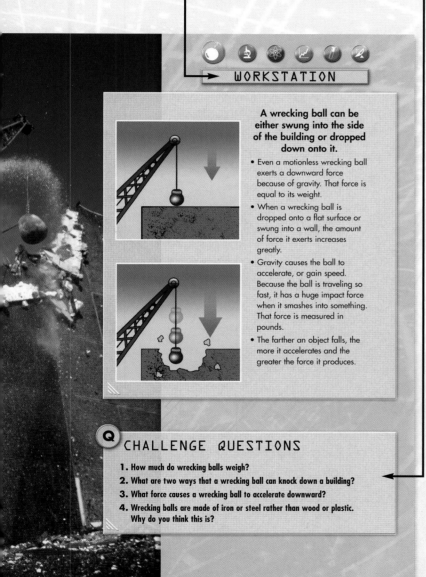

WORKSTATION

A wrecking ball can be either swung into the side of the building or dropped down onto it.

- Even a motionless wrecking ball exerts a downward force because of gravity. That force is equal to its weight.
- When a wrecking ball is dropped onto a flat surface or swung into a wall, the amount of force it exerts increases greatly.
- Gravity causes the ball to accelerate, or gain speed. Because the ball is traveling so fast, it has a huge impact force when it smashes into something. That force is measured in pounds.
- The farther an object falls, the more it accelerates and the greater the force it produces.

Q CHALLENGE QUESTIONS

1. How much do wrecking balls weigh?
2. What are two ways that a wrecking ball can knock down a building?
3. What force causes a wrecking ball to accelerate downward?
4. Wrecking balls are made of iron or steel rather than wood or plastic. Why do you think this is?

13

IF YOU NEED HELP!

TIPS FOR SCIENCE SUCCESS

On page 30, you will find tips to help you with your science work.

ANSWERS

Turn to page 31 to check your answers. (*Try all the activities and questions before you take a look at the answers.*)

GLOSSARY

Turn to page 32 for definitions of demolition words and science words.

WHAT GOES UP...

You're a demolition engineer, and you've just been given your first big project. You have been asked to demolish two buildings. One is a 15-story steel-frame office building. The other is an 18-story apartment building built with reinforced concrete. Like most demolition engineers, you've trained on the job. You've learned that it takes a lot more than explosives to bring down a building safely. Now you're ready to test your skills. So let's get to it!

FACTFILE

There are various reasons for demolishing buildings and other structures.

- Some are old and in danger of collapsing without warning.
- Others have been damaged by a fire or an earthquake and are beyond repair.
- Some are simply no longer useful.

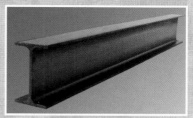

Before you can think about demolishing buildings, you need to understand how they have been built. Most large buildings are made of either steel or reinforced concrete.

A steel girder

Steel-reinforced concrete

STEEL BUILDINGS

- The 15-story office building is a steel building.
- Steel buildings are made from heavy steel girders bolted or welded together. Concrete is poured at the base of each story to make the floor. The outer covering of the building is usually glass.
- The girders supporting the building are hidden inside it. The outer walls do not bear the weight of the building. They are called curtain walls.

REINFORCED CONCRETE BUILDINGS

- The apartment building is made of reinforced concrete.
- Reinforced concrete contains steel rods, known as rebar (short for reinforcing bars). Rebar greatly strengthens a concrete structure.
- Liquid concrete is poured around rebar when a building is being built. The concrete hardens around the rods.

The force of gravity pulls objects toward the center of the Earth. Gravity will pull any object down. A building that can support itself against the forces that push and pull on it has structural integrity.

- The strong columns of a building provide a balancing force that opposes gravity. This gives the building structural integrity.
- A building stands because it has balanced forces. As long as gravity is balanced by structural integrity, a building will not fall.
- Demolition engineers may weaken the columns of buildings with explosives. This allows them to use gravity to take down the building.

GRAVITY

A building's structural integrity helps it resist forces such as gravity.

Q CHALLENGE QUESTIONS

1. Give three reasons why a building might need to be destroyed.
2. How can a concrete wall be made stronger?
3. What stops tall buildings from collapsing due to gravity?
4. How do demolition engineers sometimes use gravity to destroy buildings?

You've arrived at the 15-story steel-frame office building. You and your team make a careful inspection of a building, inside and out. You must decide exactly how to proceed with the demolition. You first need to decide whether to use mechanical methods or explosives. Mechanical demolition uses large machines to cut, crush, or knock down buildings. Explosive demolition uses controlled blasting to make buildings implode, or fall straight down, rather than exploding outward.

Demolition engineers need to gather as much information as they can about a building. They look carefully at blueprints. These are detailed plans that show the layout of a building.

FACTFILE

Implosion can mean two different things.

- In science, the word implosion means an inward collapse caused by outside pressure, such as air or water pressure.
- In demolition, a building implosion is a vertical collapse caused by gravity.

Mechanical Demolition

Most buildings are demolished with mechanical methods.

- For buildings up to about 15 stories high, mechanical methods are usually the best choice.
- If a building is very close to other buildings, explosives may cause damage to the other buildings. In that case, mechanical methods may also be the best choice.

Explosive Demolition

Only about one building in 100 is destroyed with explosives.

- There are no set rules for when explosives are used. They are often the best option for tall buildings. It is hard for machines to reach buildings taller than 15 stories.
- If there is little or no room for wrecking machines to move around a building, then explosives may be the only option.
- Sometimes buildings as low as eight stories are brought down with explosives. This is because explosive demolition is quicker than mechanical demolition.

Q CHALLENGE QUESTIONS

Below are descriptions of four buildings. Would you use mechanical or explosive demolition to bring each one down?

1. An office building that is 55 stories high
2. A school that stands between two other structures: an old church and a library. Both buildings are close by.
3. A 15-story apartment building. It has a parking lot at the back of the building and a wide driveway in front.
4. A building that is 10 stories high. Construction of a new building on the same site needs to start very soon.

TOXIC MATERIALS

Work has begun on the office building. You instruct the demolition team to start removing doors, windows, and other things inside the office building that are not part of the structure that supports it. This process is called soft strip. Workers wearing protective clothing also take out potentially harmful materials. This work will go on for several weeks before demolition can begin.

The workers soft stripping this building wear face masks to keep them from breathing in poisonous materials.

FACTFILE

- Buildings constructed before the 1970s often contain toxic, or poisonous, materials. Before then, no one knew the materials were harmful. Most are no longer used.

- A mineral called asbestos and chemicals called PCBs were both used in insulation. Insulation helps keep heat or electricity from escaping from pipes or wires. Asbestos and PCBs seemed to be ideal insulation materials, because both are fireproof and unaffected by high temperatures.

Before a building can be demolished, it must be inspected for harmful waste.

- Harmful materials must be very carefully removed and disposed of.
- Dangerous materials must be removed before a building is demolished. If they weren't removed, the materials would escape in a toxic cloud when the building collapsed. That could harm people who live or work nearby.

This chart lists the most common toxic materials found in older buildings.

This symbol is used to warn people that a material is toxic.

TOXIC MATERIALS

	Material	Used in	Effects
	Asbestos	Insulation materials	Scarring of the lungs; lung cancer
	Lead	Paints, pipes	Blood diseases; kidney damage; nerve and brain damage
	Mercury	Paints	Skin disorders; rashes; kidney damage; nerve damage
	PCBs	Electrical equipment	Skin, nose, and lung irritations; cancer

Q CHALLENGE QUESTIONS

1. How do demolition workers protect themselves from toxic substances?
2. Why were asbestos and PCBs once widely used in insulation?
3. Which toxic substances were once used in paint?
4. A demolition worker develops a skin rash and nerve problems. Which toxic substance might have caused these health problems?
5. Why is it important to remove toxic substances from a building before demolishing it?

WRECKING BALL

Now that the office building is completely safe, you can begin demolition. You have decided to knock down the top floors with a wrecking ball. This is a huge iron weight suspended on a cable from a tall crane. Operating a wrecking ball requires great skill. Your operator is one of the best in the business. As the wrecking ball delivers crushing blows to the top floors, the scattered pieces of the building fall from the upper stories onto the ground.

FACTFILE

Wrecking balls can weigh from two to five tons.

When the wrecking ball is released, it is pulled down by gravity. As it moves down, the chain pulls it forward.

The ball continues to swing forward and upward. It is propelled by its own weight and speed. Weight and speed together give the ball a force of movement called momentum.

A wrecking ball can be either swung into the side of the building or dropped down onto it.

- Even a motionless wrecking ball exerts a downward force because of gravity. That force is equal to its weight.

- When a wrecking ball is dropped onto a flat surface or swung into a wall, the amount of force it exerts increases greatly.

- Gravity causes the ball to accelerate, or gain speed. Because the ball is traveling so fast, it has a huge impact force when it smashes into something. That force is measured in pounds.

- The farther an object falls, the more it accelerates and the greater the force it produces.

Q CHALLENGE QUESTIONS

1. How much do wrecking balls weigh?

2. What are two ways that a wrecking ball can knock down a building?

3. What force causes a wrecking ball to accelerate downward?

4. Wrecking balls are made of iron or steel rather than wood or plastic. Why do you think this is?

HYDRAULIC EXCAVATORS

The top five stories of the office building are now gone. You decide that the wrecking ball has done enough work on the building. It's time to bring in the real monsters of demolition: hydraulic excavators. These machines are like huge metal dinosaurs. They have parts that can cut, chew, or smash any building material. Excavators use hundreds of tons of force to do their job. On these pages, you will learn how they work!

FACTFILE

When you push on something, you are adding a force to the object. This force creates pressure. Putting pressure on the surface of a liquid, such as water, makes the liquid want to move away from the pressure. Think of a tube of toothpaste. You squeeze it at one end and the toothpaste squirts out the other end. You are applying pressure.

Hydraulic systems use a solid cylinder called a piston to push against liquid inside a tube. This pressure generates the force needed to move the excavator's arm. Hydraulic excavators use cylinders of different sizes to increase the force they can apply.

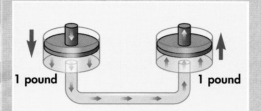

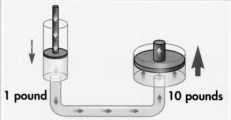

- The two pistons in this picture are the same size. If you apply a downward force of one pound to one piston, an upward force of one pound will push against the other piston.

- The pistons will move the same distance. If one moves down an inch, the other will move up an inch.

- Here the piston on the right has 10 times the surface area of the piston on the left. Surface area means the surface on which the fluid can push.

- If you apply a downward force to the left piston, a force 10 times greater will push against the right piston. The right piston moves only one-tenth the distance you pushed the left piston.

How the Hydraulic Excavator's Arm Works

- Your arm bends and moves at joints at the shoulder, elbow, and wrist. The hydraulic excavator's arm is put together in a similar way, but it has a claw or scoop instead of a hand. Instead of muscles, the excavator has hydraulic systems that make it move.

- Hydraulic systems move things by applying pressure to fluid in a tube or cylinder.

- A small force is applied to the fluid in the narrow tubes on the arm. That force is transferred to a larger cylinder bolted to the arm.

- The greater force of the piston in the large cylinder moves the arm.

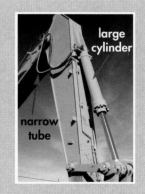

Q CHALLENGE QUESTIONS

Piston B has a surface area 10 times larger than Piston A.

1. How far will Piston A have to move for Piston B to move 3 inches?

2. If Piston A is pushed down with a force of 4 pounds, how much upward force will apply to Piston B?

3. If Piston B has an upward force of 20 pounds, how much force was applied to Piston A?

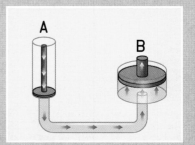

OPERATING AN EXCAVATOR

You've learned how to work an excavator, so you can take the controls of one of these machines. It's a big yellow monster fitted with a powerful fast-moving hammer called a hydraulic breaker. You control the excavator with a pair of joysticks and two foot pedals. You pull one of the joysticks back to raise the excavator's arm. Then, by pressing a button on the stick, you start the hydraulic breaker. You watch as it smashes through the concrete walls of the building.

This is the hydraulic breaker.

You use the joysticks to swing the excavator's cab around. They also control the long, jointed arm, called the boom, and operate the breaker.

You move the machine on its tracks using the levers, or foot pedals.

There are excavator attachments for just about every demolition task. These are a few of the attachments commonly used on demolition projects.

Shears can cut through just about anything, including steel beams that are 6 inches (15 centimeters) thick.

Hydraulic breakers pound apart stone or concrete surfaces.

Grapple jaws are used for grabbing and moving heavy objects.

Pulverizers are used to crush and tear apart low walls and floors.

scissors = small surface area

pliers = large surface area

Some excavator attachments exert a shearing force. Others exert a crushing force.

- Shears act like giant scissors. They exert a great deal of force along a narrow line. This enables them to cut cleanly through thick metal or other materials.

- Pulverizers are similar to pliers. Their force is spread across a wider surface, so they can crush and grind materials into pieces rather than slicing them apart.

Q CHALLENGE QUESTIONS

1. Which attachment would you use to smash apart a concrete sidewalk?
2. Which attachment would you use to transport large rocks at a site and stack them up?
3. What would be your best choice for cutting through heavy metal pipes?
4. Which two attachments would both be good for demolishing concrete floors in a building?
5. If a tool applies force to a large surface area, is it best for crushing or cutting?

DEBRIS AND RECYCLING

Hauling away the debris that piles up is an important part of a demolition project. You make sure that your workers separate out any items or materials that can be reused or recycled. This is good for the environment. It's good for you, too. You get money for materials that can be recycled. The remaining debris is taken to a landfill.

FACTFILE

Here are some of the benefits of reuse and recycling.

- Less landfill space is needed.
- Less air and ground pollution is created by rotting debris in landfills.
- Reusing construction materials means fewer new materials will need to be made. This saves energy.
- Less air pollution is created by factories, because they do not have to make as many new construction materials.

WORKSTATION

This pie chart shows how much of each material is found in demolition debris.

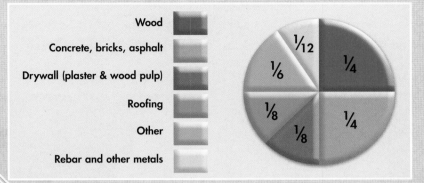

Wood
Concrete, bricks, asphalt
Drywall (plaster & wood pulp)
Roofing
Other
Rebar and other metals

$\frac{1}{12}$ $\frac{1}{4}$ $\frac{1}{6}$ $\frac{1}{8}$ $\frac{1}{8}$ $\frac{1}{4}$

What happens to demolition debris?

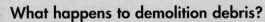

- Useful items, such as doors and sinks, are almost always saved and resold.
- Wood is often reused in construction or turned into wood chips.
- Bricks are cleaned for reuse in new buildings.
- Concrete is ground up and used in asphalt for road construction.
- Rebar and other metals are melted and recycled into new metal items.

How much of demolition debris is recycled?

In the United States, only about one-quarter of the debris from demolition sites is recycled. The rest goes to landfills. In England, about one-half of debris from demolition sites is recycled. However, it is estimated that three-quarters of the debris from demolition could be reused or recycled.

Q CHALLENGE QUESTIONS

1. Roofing makes up what fraction of demolition debris?
2. How does recycling demolition debris help reduce air pollution?
3. Which country recycles a greater fraction of its demolition debris: the U.S. or England?
4. Which material from demolition is used for building new roads?

PLANNING AN EXPLOSION

While the demolition of the office building proceeds, you begin to plan the demolition of the apartment building. You decide to use explosives. The apartment building has other buildings around it, so you must make sure that it falls straight down. The goal is to weaken the structure and let gravity do the rest. The building should collapse under its own weight. If this is done correctly, the building will fall in the right direction.

Safety is important at a demolition site. Workers must wear hard hats and reflective jackets.

When a building is imploded, it is often best to have it fall within its footprint.

- A building's footprint is the area it occupies on the ground.

- The Kingdome in Seattle, Washington, (shown left) fell almost perfectly within its footprint when it was imploded in 2000.

- All implosions involve a number of explosions. These occur in a carefully planned order. The entire process, however, usually takes less than 30 seconds.

By detonating, or setting off, explosives in a planned order, you can control the way a building falls.

- To make a building fall in a certain direction, you set off explosives at the bottom of that side first. That weakens the building's supports. The building leans in the direction you want. Other explosions throughout the building will bring the whole structure down in that direction.

- To make a building fall inward, you need to set off explosives in the middle of the building first. That makes the outside walls fall inward.

- The last explosives to be set off are usually those on the upper floors of the building. That makes the building collapse in a controlled way.

CHALLENGE QUESTIONS

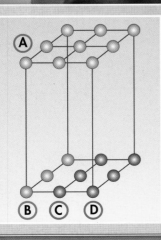

Your team has placed explosives at the points labeled A, B, C, and D on the building shown here.

1. In which direction will gravity cause the building to fall if you set off the explosives labeled D first?

2. If you wanted the building to fall into an empty lot to the left, which set of explosives would you set off first?

3. There are buildings to both the left and right. Which explosives would you want to set off first?

4. Which set of explosives would you set off last?

21

PLACING EXPLOSIVES

You help the demolition crew prepare the apartment building for the implosion. The crew uses sledgehammers to knock down the nonsupporting walls in the building. This will make sure that the building collapses properly. Then you supervise as the crew drills holes in the columns and walls that support the building. Your team carefully places sticks of dynamite in those holes.

You plant explosives in the building's columns. Then you wrap the columns to keep debris from flying out.

FACTFILE

There are two main kinds of explosives.

- **High explosives,** such as dynamite, explode with enough force to destroy the building's supports. High explosives are difficult to ignite, however.

- **Low explosives** burn more slowly but are easier to ignite. They are often used to help light high explosives.

When planning an implosion, you do test blasts on columns in the building. This helps you decide how much dynamite you will need to demolish the building.

Columns are wrapped in heavy fabrics before the test blast. This holds in the debris during the explosion.

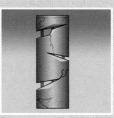

This column was blown up with too little dynamite.

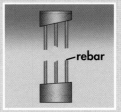

This column was destroyed with the correct amount of explosives.

TOOLS OF A BLASTER

Blasting machine
By pressing a button on this device, you send an electrical charge that sets off a single detonating cap.

Detonating cords
The blaster is attached to cords that are filled with an explosive. An explosion travels down each cord and triggers the blasting caps.

Blasting caps
These low explosives are used to ignite, or start, larger explosives, such as sticks of dynamite.

High explosives
Dynamite can shatter concrete. For steel columns, you must use more powerful high explosives.

Q CHALLENGE QUESTIONS

1. Why is it necessary to wrap concrete columns with heavy materials for a test blast?
2. What kind of explosives would you use to implode a steel-frame building?
3. What do you think will happen to the building if you used too much explosive? What if you use too little?
4. Why do experts often use both low explosives and high explosives to implode a building?

23

PROTECTING THE PUBLIC

You are now four months into the project. In the apartment building, the crew is making final preparations for the implosion, which is scheduled for later today. You walk through the building to make one last inspection. Everything looks good. There's a feeling of excitement in the air. The area for several blocks around has been cleared of people. From a safe distance, crowds are gathering to watch the implosion.

FACTFILE

You have taken steps to protect nearby houses and underground water, gas, and telephone lines.

- The nearby houses have been covered with material to protect them from flying debris and dust.

- The gas and water lines near the building have been covered with large mounds of soil. This will cushion them from the impact of debris hitting the ground.

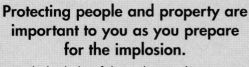

Protecting people and property are important to you as you prepare for the implosion.

- With the help of the police and security guards, you move everyone out of the area for a distance of three blocks. The police have closed all the surrounding streets to traffic.

FAMOUS IMPLOSIONS

The amount of explosive needed to destroy a building depends on many things, including its height and construction material.

Building and Location	Year demolished	Height	Construction material	Pounds of explosives used
J. L. Hudson Department Store, Detroit, Michigan	1998	21 stories	Steel	2,728
Mendes Caldeira Building, Sao Paolo, Brazil	1975	32 stories	Reinforced concrete	1,000
Biltmore Hotel, Oklahoma City, Oklahoma	1977	28 stories	Steel	800
Philips Building, Oslo, Norway	2000	15 stories	Reinforced concrete	220

Q CHALLENGE QUESTIONS

1. Why are nearby houses covered up before the implosion?
2. Look at the chart above. Which building required the most explosives?
3. How much taller was the Mendes Caldeira Building than the Philips Building?
4. Does a taller building always require more explosives than a smaller building? Explain your answer.

A REAL BLAST!

The time has come for the implosion of the apartment building. You make one final check to make sure that no one is inside the danger zone. The crowds watch silently. You and your crew have retreated to a safe distance. Now, the countdown begins: ten, nine, eight... When the count reaches zero, the blaster turns a switch on the blasting machine. Immediately, you hear a number of sharp pops as the detonating cords ignite. Those sounds are followed by loud booms, like fireworks, as the dynamite explodes. The building shakes and then crashes to the ground in a huge cloud of dust. A perfect job!

WORKSTATION

What happens in an explosion?

- An explosion is a form of combustion, or burning.
- Combustion is a chemical reaction that occurs when a material combines with oxygen. It gives off energy in the form of heat, light, and gases.
- Combustion happens at different rates. A log in a fireplace burns slowly. An explosive material, such as dynamite, has a very fast combustion rate.

A log in a fireplace may take an hour or more to burn. It releases energy and gases slowly.

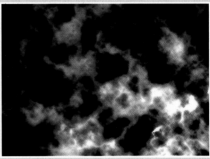

A stick of dynamite combusts within a fraction of a second. In that instant, it releases a great amount of energy and gas.

shock wave   expanding gas

heat and light   pressure

The gas released by an explosive expands rapidly.

- The explosion produces a shock wave that puts a huge amount of pressure on surrounding objects.
- This tremendous pressure causes the most damage in an explosion. It can knock down or tear apart nearby objects. This kind of force can shatter concrete and rip steel apart.

Q CHALLENGE QUESTIONS

1. Combustion is a chemical reaction that occurs when a material combines with which gas?
2. What kinds of energy are released during combustion?
3. Which has the faster rate of combustion: a burning log or dynamite?
4. What causes the most damage to objects in an explosion: light, heat, or pressure?

WRAPPING IT UP

The dust is settling in the area around the imploded apartment building. Only the crumbled remains of the building are left. Tomorrow you will put excavators with concrete-pulverizing jaws to work on the rubble. They will break the concrete into small pieces and remove the rebar for recycling. The concrete will be sold to a construction company that builds roads. Everything has worked out well. Best of all, no one was hurt. You'll be back on the job tomorrow, but for now everyone has earned a good night's rest.

FACTFILE

- A major health concern from demolition is dust, which can cause a number of health problems if people breathe it in.

- During a mechanical demolition project, workers often use fire hoses to wet down debris. The water turns the dust to mud, which doesn't float in the air as dust does. That reduces the amount of dust that people might breathe in.

It is almost impossible to prevent a huge cloud of dust from rising during an implosion.

- When the building collapses, air in the building is forced out in a great blast of wind. That wind carries a huge amount of dust with it.

- Dust from concrete and bricks contains a substance called silica. Silica can damage the lungs, even if breathed in for only a short time.

- Workers can protect themselves by wearing masks over their mouth and nose. The masks are made with a fine mesh. The mesh lets in air, but pieces of silica are too large to pass through it.

After the implosion, you must make sure that the site is safe before anyone returns to it.

- You watch videos showing the implosion of the building from several angles. You want to see where the explosives went off.

- You compare the videos to your plans. Did all of the explosives in the building go off?

- Any explosives that did not go off must be removed by experts. Otherwise, they could go off unexpectedly and cause injury.

- You must check that the building has fully collapsed. You want to make sure there is no danger of any further collapse.

Q CHALLENGE QUESTIONS

1. How does spraying water on demolition debris keep dust to a minimum?
2. What is silica?
3. Why do workers at demolition sites wear face masks?
4. Why is it important to watch the explosion of a building from all angles on video?
5. What steps do you take to protect people after a building has imploded?

Pages 10–11

Toxic Materials

Demolition workers aren't the only people who are sometimes exposed to dangerous substances. People who live in old houses can be surrounded by the same sorts of dangers. For example, lead-based paint was used a lot in past decades. When stripping off very old paint, people should find out what kind of paint it is. If it contains lead, they need to wear a protective face mask as they strip the paint.

Pages 12–13

Wrecking Ball

Because weight is a type of force, you are exerting a downward force every time you stand on something. If a bathroom scale says you weigh 100 pounds, that means you are exerting 100 pounds of downward force on the scale.

Pages 14–15

Hydraulic Excavators

A fluid is any substance that has no fixed shape and flows easily. Both gases and liquids are fluids. The fluids used in hydraulic devices, however, are all liquids. Unlike gases, liquids cannot be compressed. Pressure simply squeezes gases so they take up less space. But when you put pressure on a fluid, that pressure is transferred throughout the liquid.

Pages 24–25

Protecting the Public

There is no simple formula for the amount of explosives needed for a building implosion. It depends on three main factors:

- The height of the building.
- The width and depth of the building. A short building can still be very wide!
- The materials, such as steel or concrete, that were used to build it.

Pages 28–29

Wrapping It Up

Very fine dust is dangerous because it can be breathed into the lungs, where it stays. Silica in dust can cause a disease called silicosis. It causes scar tissue to form in the lungs, which makes it hard to breathe. There is no cure for silicosis.

Pages 6–7

1. It may be old or in danger of collapsing; it could have been damaged by a fire or earthquake; or it could just be no longer useful.
2. Rebar (reinforcing bars) makes a concrete wall much stronger.
3. Buildings are kept from collapsing by their structural integrity.
4. Engineers weaken the columns of a building, so the building is pulled down by gravity.

Pages 8–9

1. 1. Explosive demolition, 2. Mechanical demolition, 3. Mechanical demolition, 4. Explosive demolition

Pages 10–11

1. They wear protective clothing and use face masks to avoid breathing in toxic substances.
2. They are resistant to high temperatures.
3. Lead and mercury
4. Mercury
5. Demolition would release a toxic cloud of chemicals that could harm people nearby.

Pages 12–13

1. Two to five tons
2. A wrecking ball can be swung into the side of a building or dropped down on to it.
3. Gravity
4. Iron and steel are heavy and hard. They produce a bigger impact force than plastic or wood.

Pages 14–15

1. 30 inches
2. 40 pounds
3. 2 pounds

Pages 16–17

1. A hydraulic breaker
2. Grapple jaws
3. Shears
4. The hydraulic breaker and pulverizer
5. Crushing

Pages 18–19

1. 1/8
2. Less air pollution is created by rotting debris, and factories produce less air pollution because they do not have to manufacture as many new construction materials.
3. England
4. Concrete

Pages 20–21

1. The building would fall to the right.
2. B
3. You would set off the explosives labeled C first.
4. A

Pages 22–23

1. Engineers want to stop debris from flying out and hurting people and damaging other buildings.
2. Powerful explosives
3. If you use too much explosive, flying debris may cause damage to nearby buildings. If not enough explosive is used, the building may not collapse.
4. Low explosives, such as blasting caps, are used to ignite high explosives, such as dynamite.

Pages 24–25

1. To protect them from flying debris and dust
2. The J. L. Hudson Department Store
3. 17 stories taller
4. No. The Mendes Caldeira Building and the Biltmore Hotel were both taller than the J. L. Hudson Department Store, but required less explosives.

Pages 26–27

1. Oxygen
2. Light and heat
3. Dynamite
4. Pressure

Pages 28–29

1. Wet dust becomes mud, which doesn't float in the air, so cannot be breathed in.
2. A substance found in the dust of concrete and bricks that can cause lung problems
3. To protect their lungs from demolition dust, including silica
4. You need to make sure that all the explosives have gone off. There is a danger that explosives could still be in the rubble. The explosives could go off without warning and hurt people.
5. Keep people away from the site; make sure the building is fully collapsed and that there are no explosives left that have not gone off.

GLOSSARY

ASPHALT a road surface made of crushed rock, concrete, and tar

BLUEPRINT a detailed plan for a project

COMBUSTION the process of catching fire and burning

DEBRIS the remains of something that has been destroyed

DECAY to rot and break down over time

DEMOLISH to knock down or destroy something

DETONATE to make something explode

EXCAVATOR a person or a machine that helps demolish a building

EXPLOSION a sudden and violent chemical reaction in which heat, light and pressure are released

FLUID a substance that has no fixed shape and flows easily. Gases and liquids are both fluids.

FOOTPRINT the amount of space an object covers

GIRDER a long metal beam that is used to support a building

HYDRAULIC PRESSURE a pressure force that is transmitted through a liquid in a tube

IGNITE to catch fire or explode

IMPACT FORCE the force exerted by a heavy object, such as a wrecking ball when it slams into a surface.

IMPLOSION in science, this means the inward collapse of an object from outside pressure. In demolition, implosion is the vertical collapse caused by gravity.

INSULATION materials that stop heat and electricity from escaping

LANDFILL an area where garbage is buried and then covered with soil

MOMENTUM the speed and weight of an object. The more momentum an object has, the harder it is to stop.

PISTON a cylinder that can be moved up and down inside a tube to put pressure on a fluid

PRESSURE the force of something pressing against something else

REBAR short for reinforcing bars; steel rods used in reinforced concrete to strengthen it

SHOCK WAVE a wave of fast-moving air or liquid.

TOXIC harmful to living things

PICTURE CREDITS

(t = top; b = bottom; c = center; l = left; r = right; f = far)

Cover: Uwe Walz/Corbis. **AFP/Getty:** 22–23 (main). **Alamy:** 20–21 (main). **Brandenburg Industrial Service Company:** 23bl. **Construction Photography:** 12–13 (main). **Corbis:** 21tc, 24–25 (main), 28–29 (main). **Englo:** 23cfl. **Getty Images:** 8–9 (main), 23cl. **Inmalo/MBI:** 17tl, 17tcr, 17tr. **iStockPhoto:** 11cl, 15cr, 27cr, 28br, 29tr. **JCB:** title page, 14–15 (main), 16–17 (foreground main), 18–19 (main), 19bl, 30–31 (main), 30bl, 31tl. **Liebherr:** 30tl. **New Holland:** 17tcl. **Science Photo Library:** 10–11 (main), 10–11tl, 23cfr. **Shutterstock:** 6–7 (main), 7tl, 9tl, 9c, 11cl, 16–17 (background main) 17c (2 images), 25tl, 26–27 (main), 26tl, 27cl, 27tl, 29cr, 29cl, 30tr, 30br. **ticktock media archive:** 7cl, 7br, 11c (4 images in chart), 12cl, 12bl, 13tl (2 images), 15br, 15tl, 15tr, 19tr, 21bl, 23tl, 23tc, 23tr. **Wikimedia:** 23cr.

Every effort has been made to trace the copyright holders, and we apologize in advance for any unintentional omissions. We would be pleased to insert the appropriate acknowledgments in any subsequent edition of this publication.